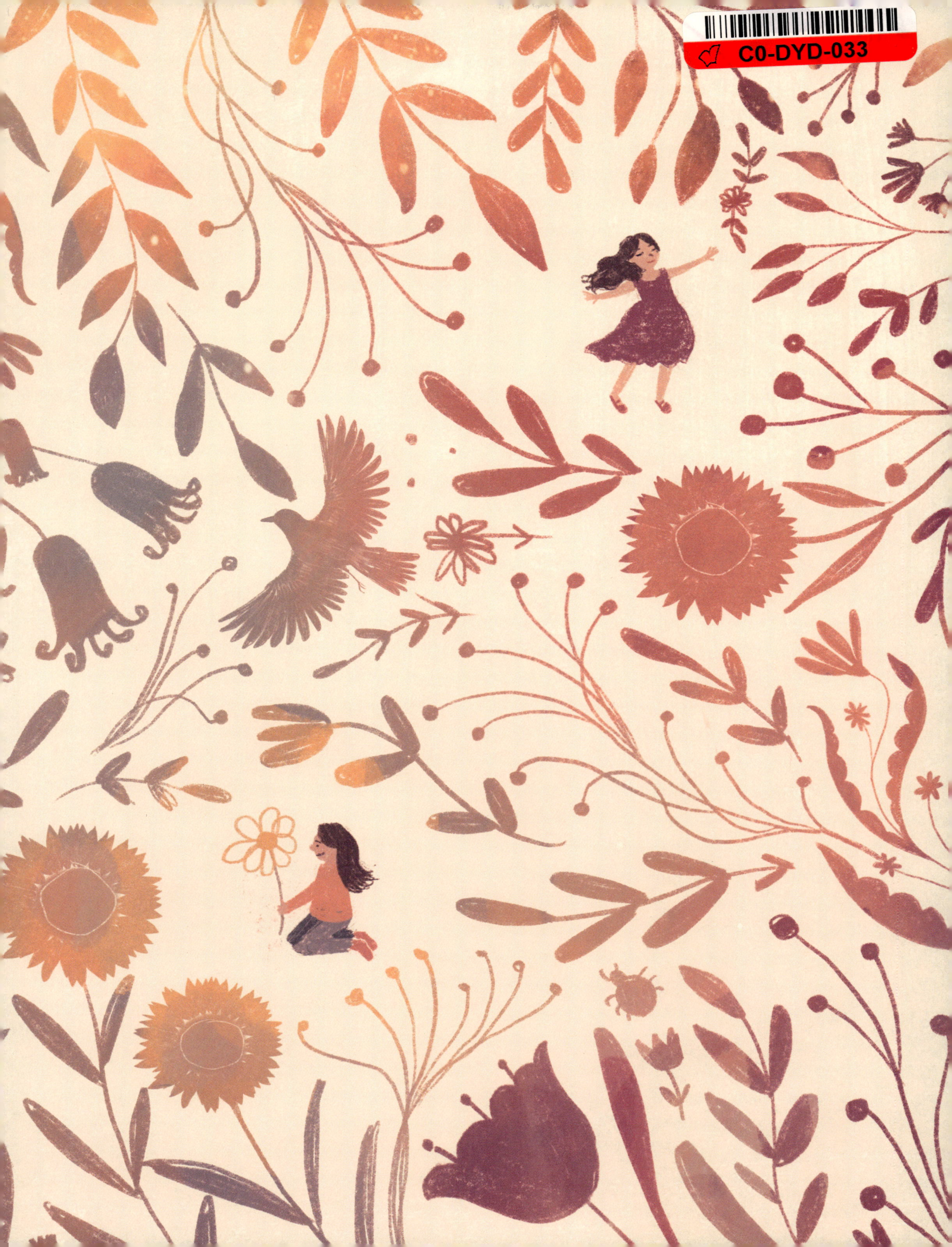

Dear Mama God

written by **DANEEN AKERS**

illustrated by **GILLIAN GAMBLE**

Watchfire
MEDIA

*For Lucy, whose prayers to Mama God
inspired this book.* —D. A.

For Hannah —G. G.

Library of Congress Control Number: 2022918002

Text copyright © 2023 by Daneen Akers
Illustrations copyright © 2023 by Gillian Gamble

All rights reserved.
Published in the United States by Watchfire Media.
www.watchfire.org

Dear Mama God is available at discount pricing for bulk purchases and educational needs.
For details, write to *support@watchfire.org*.

Designed by Aphelandra
Edited by Keisha E. McKenzie, Ph.D. and Jennifer Grant
With special thanks to disability advocate and consultant, Shannon Hope Dingle

Printed in Canada

Dear Mama God is FSC certified.
It is printed on chlorine-free paper made with 30% post-consumer waste.
It uses only vegetable and soy-based ink.

www.dearmamagod.com

Hardcover ISBN: 978-1-7340895-3-0
eBook ISBN: 978-1-7340895-4-7

FIRST EDITION
10 9 8 7 6 5 4 3 2

*"The Spirit of God, She has made me,
and the breath of the nursing God,
She gives me life."*

JOB 33:4

*Translation by The Rev. Wil Gafney, Ph.D.,
Professor of Hebrew Bible, Brite Divinity School,
Ft. Worth, TX; used by permission.*

Dear Mama God,

Thank you for the earth and all living things.

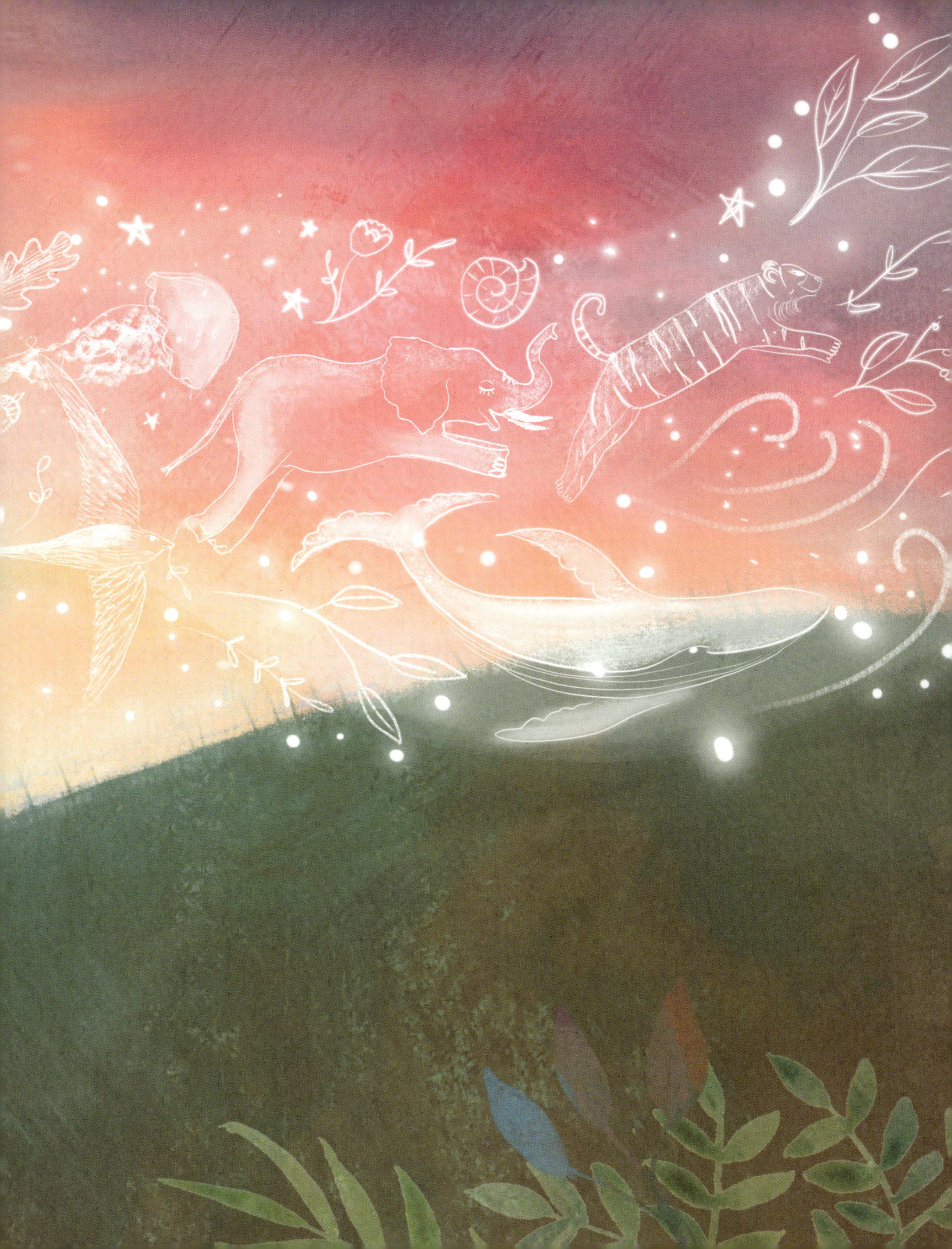

Thank you for rain
that makes rainbows.

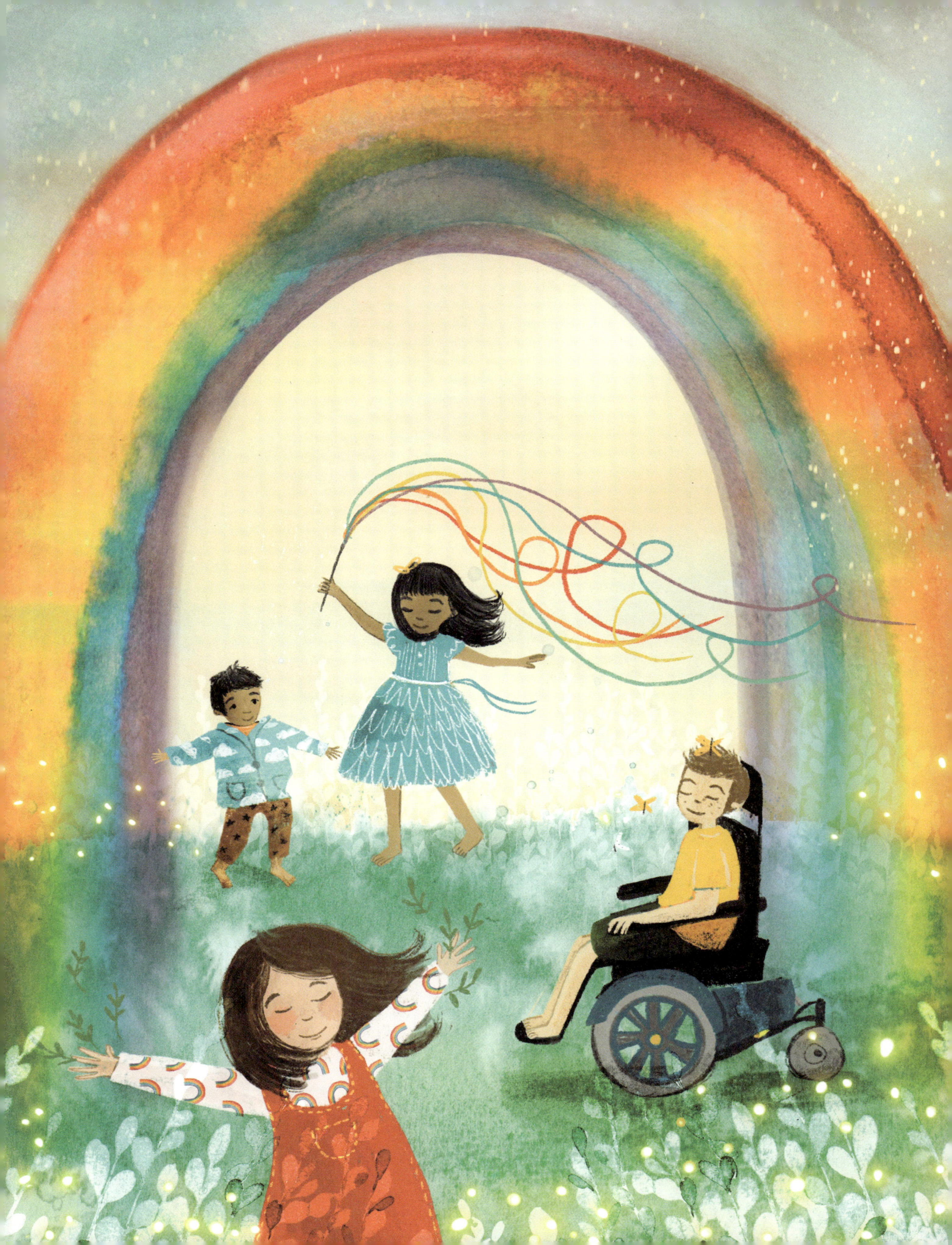

Thank you for seeds that grow into plants.

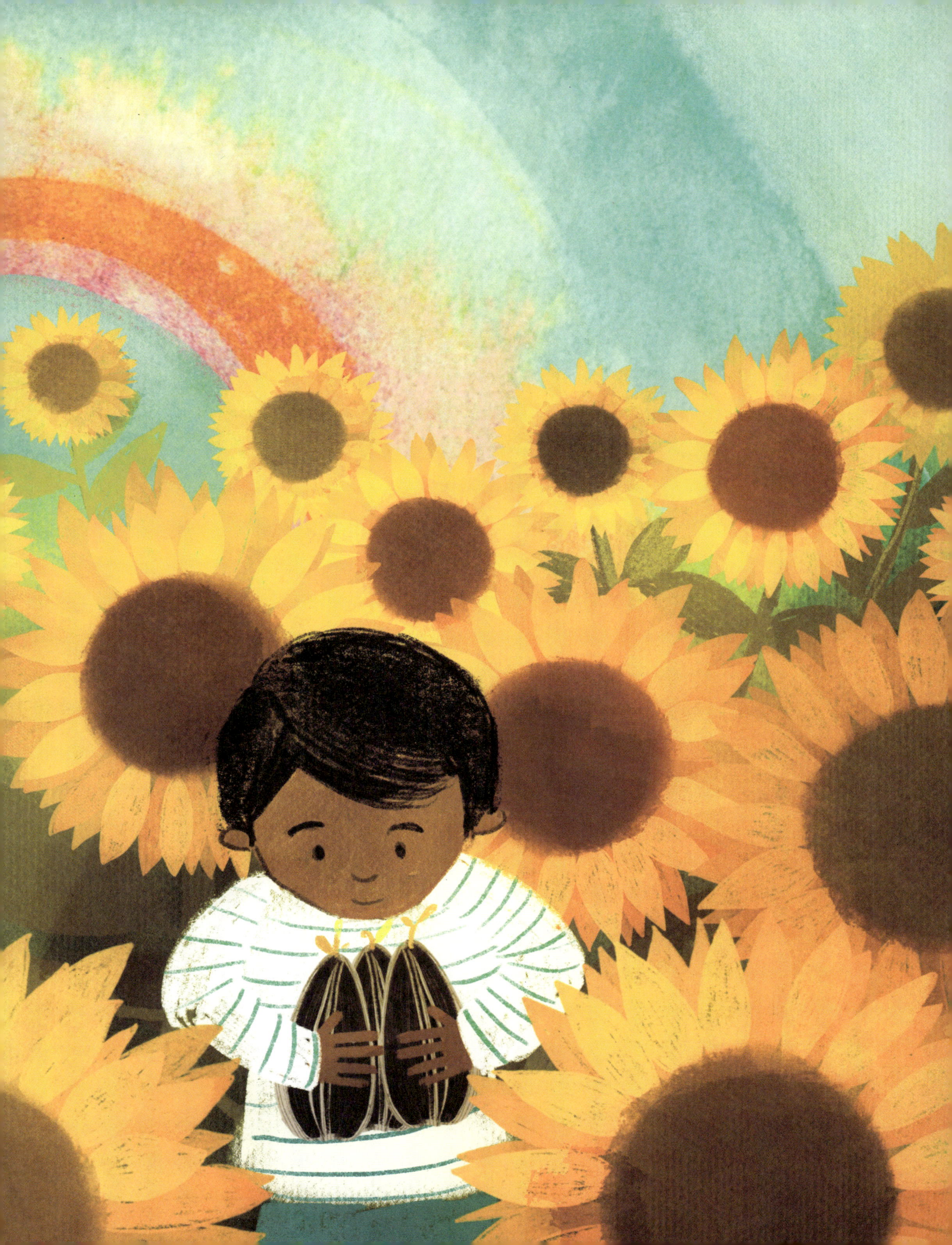

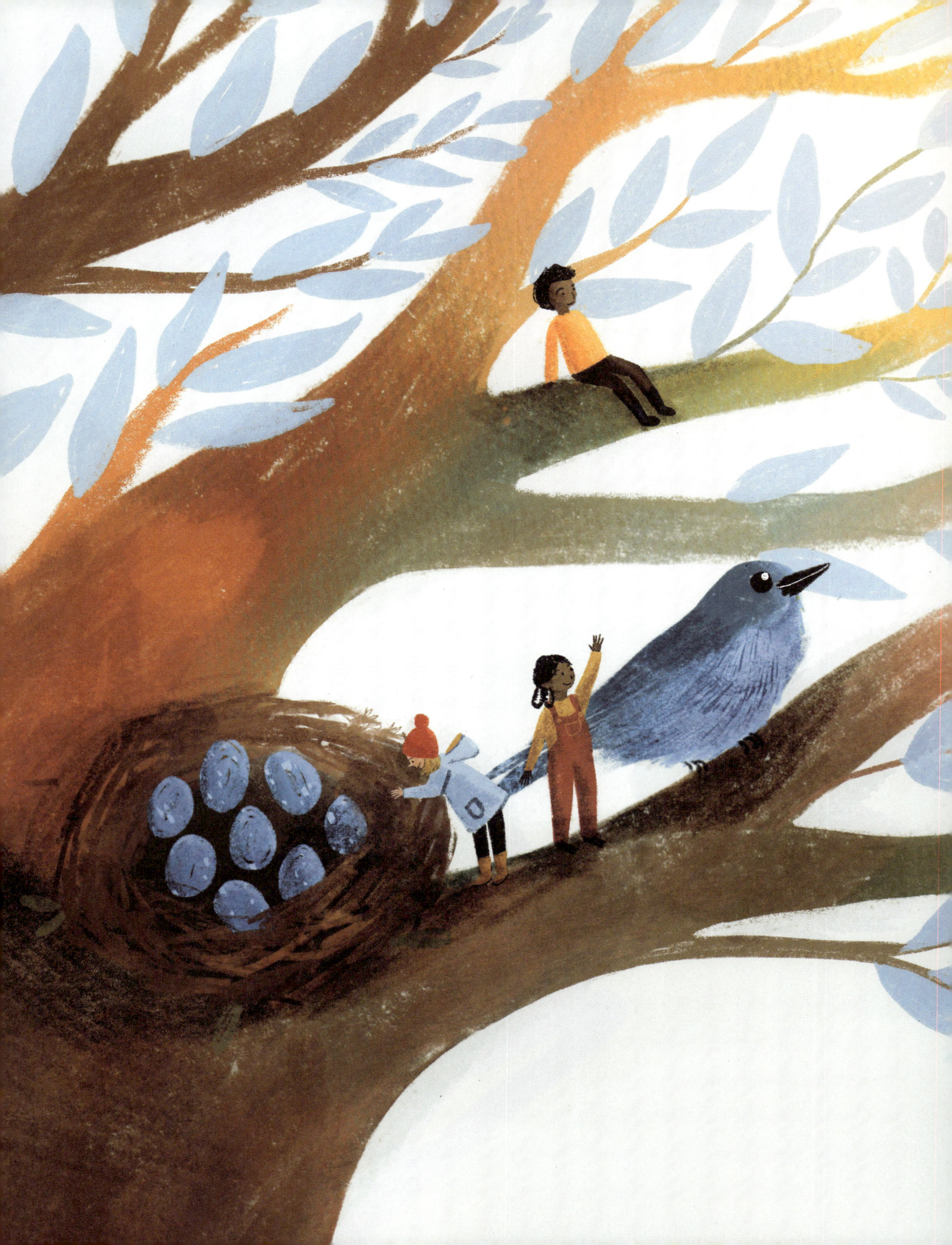

Thank you for trees for birds to build nests in.

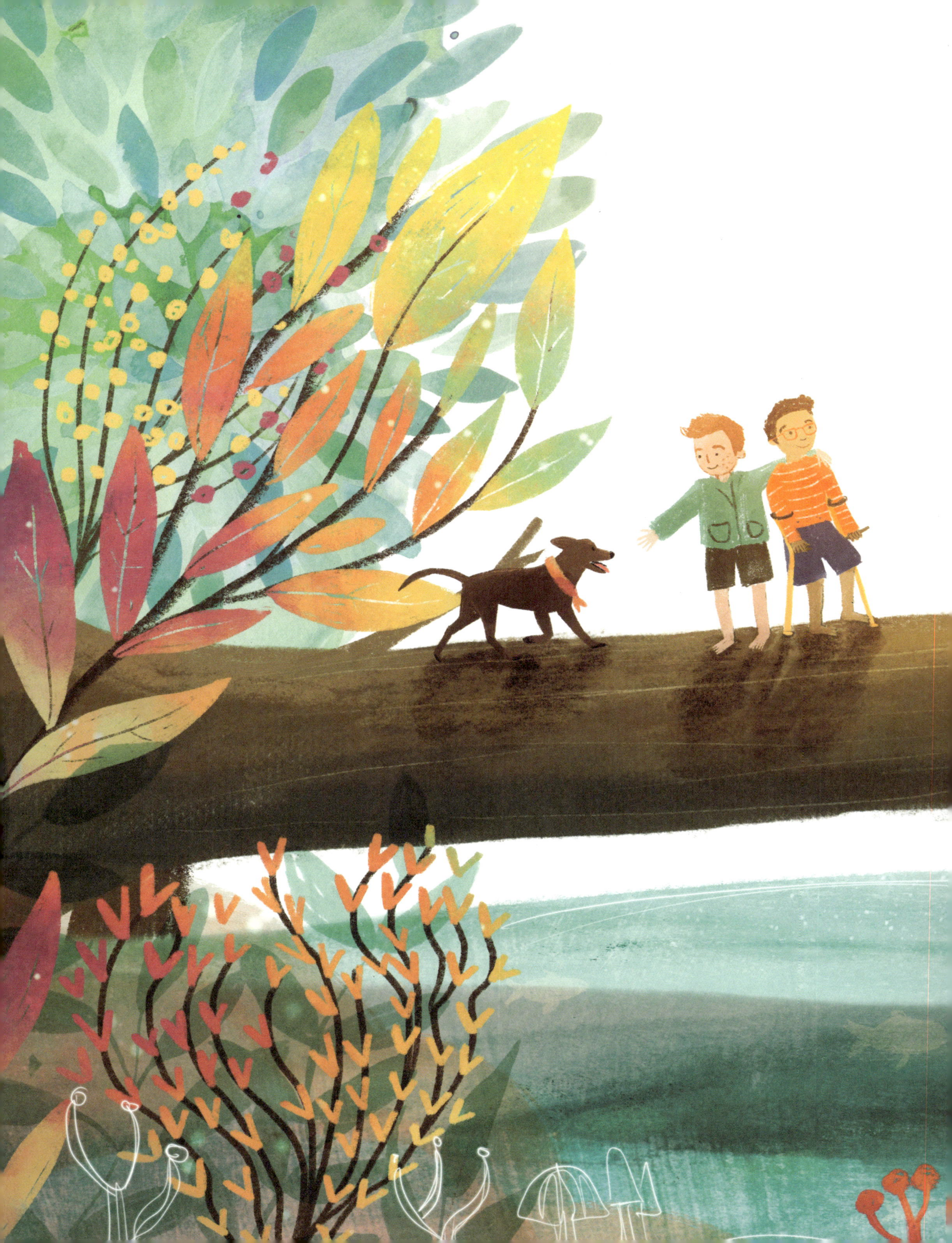

Thank you for creeks
    that flow and grow.